TEEN LIFE 411™

I HAVE
A FOOD
ALLERGY.

NOW WHAT?

JUDY MONROE PETERSON

ROSEN
PUBLISHING®

New York

Published in 2015 by The Rosen Publishing Group, Inc.
29 East 21st Street, New York, NY 10010

First Edition

Library of Congress Cataloging-in-Publication Data

Peterson, Judy Monroe, author.
I have a food allergy. Now what?/Judy Monroe Peterson.—
First edition.
        pages cm.—(Teen life 411)
Audience: Grades 7–12.
Includes bibliographical references and index.
ISBN 978-1-4777-7974-3 (library bound)
1. Food allergy—Juvenile literature. I. Title. II. Series: Teen
life 411.
RC596.P46 2014
616.97'5—dc23

                                                    2014010973

Manufactured in China

CONTENTS

If a group of teens were asked to name their favorite foods, they might say pizza, cheeseburgers, burritos, or lasagna. They may also mention cookies, cakes, candy, and ice cream. Many young people can enjoy these foods without a problem. But, for individuals with a food allergy, every mouthful can be a worry. Just a small bite of certain foods could cause them to experience mild or severe symptoms, such as rashes, itching, hives, sneezing, or wheezing. When many body systems react at the same time, someone may experience swelling of the mouth and tongue, difficulty breathing, or low blood pressure. Such serious reactions can be a threat to life itself. Fortunately, such fatal reactions to food are very rare.

Food allergies are a large health problem worldwide, affecting as many as 220 to 520 million people globally, according to the World Allergy Organization. In the United States, approximately fifteen

Peanuts, often in the form of peanut butter, are a popular and inexpensive source of dietary protein. But they are a classic allergen that affects children and adults.

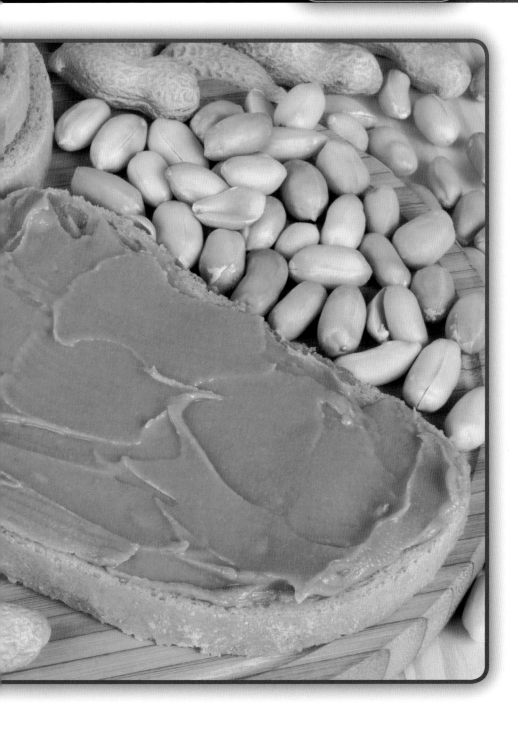

million people have a food allergy. Of that number, one out of thirteen is under the age of eighteen, which is equal to about one or two students in every classroom. Food allergies and their related severe reactions are on the rise. In 2013, the U.S. Centers for Disease Control and Prevention estimated that the number of children and teens with food allergies has nearly doubled during the last fifteen years.

People can be allergic to almost any food. Those with a food allergy cannot eat certain foods or drink specific beverages. If they do, the body's immune system attacks normally harmless substances in the foods. These substances are known as allergens, and they are usually proteins. The immune system responds to them as it would to pathogens, or disease-causing organisms, such as a cold virus, resulting in unpleasant and sometimes serious symptoms.

More than 170 foods can be allergens. According to Food Allergy Research & Education (FARE), people have had food reactions to corn, gelatin, meat, seeds (mostly sesame, sunflower, and poppy seeds), and spices (such as caraway, coriander, garlic, and mustard), but eight foods are much more likely than these to trigger an allergic reaction. The top culprits, accounting for about 90 percent of all food-related allergies, are milk, eggs, peanuts, tree nuts (including almonds, walnuts, cashews, and Brazil nuts), wheat, soy, fish, and shellfish. Someone may be allergic to only one specific food such as nuts, while another person might have multiple allergies to a variety of different foods. Here, you will learn about the eight most common food allergies.

A food allergy is unpredictable. Sometimes children and teens outgrow them, or they could last a lifetime. In addition, individuals at a later age could develop a new food allergy that never troubled them before. Although no medication exists to prevent an allergic reaction from happening in the first place, getting diagnosed correctly by an allergist is important. These doctors specialize in the treatment of allergies. They can treat various symptoms with medicines, including serious reactions.

Researchers have not found a cure for food allergies at present. Although the best way to control a food allergy is to avoid the allergen completely, that's not easy to do all day and every day. A simple event such as eating popcorn and candy at a movie, pizza or tacos at a party, or fast food at a restaurant with friends may be a concern for someone with a food allergy. However, by paying careful attention, often with the help of family and friends, most people who have food allergies can live healthy lives.

Most people enjoy eating. Although that statement is true for many teens who have a food allergy, they must be very careful. For these teens, consuming the wrong food or beverage sets off a chain of immune system responses that can make them feel sick for hours or days, or cause them to have dangerous allergic reactions. Everyone responds differently when a food allergy is triggered.

PUZZLING IMMUNE SYSTEM RESPONSE

To understand allergies, it's helpful to know about the immune system and how it functions. The immune system is made up of an essential network of cells, tissues, and organs that work together to defend the body against pathogens, such as the influenza virus, that could cause an infection. The immune system usually does a good

The intensity of an allergic reaction depends on the amount of the allergen someone has consumed and how sensitive the person is to that allergen.

job of fighting off harmful microbial invaders and other foreign substances, in steps called the immune response, with the help of special white blood cells. These cells produce antibodies that battle pathogens and allergens. The immune system makes a different antibody for every allergen it encounters.

The first time individuals eat a food they are allergic to, they may not notice any symptoms. However, the immune system's response is that the food is poisonous and is an allergen. The immune system swings into action by producing immunoglobulin E (IgE), a kind of protein called an antibody. Different IgEs match different kinds of allergens and fit together like the pieces of a jigsaw puzzle. For example, a milk allergen pairs up with one kind of IgE, while a peanut allergen corresponds with another type of IgE. Some IgEs circulate in the blood, but most stick to the surface of mast cells located in the skin, nose, throat, lungs, and stomach. Once the antibodies are in place, the mast cells are sensitized, or primed, and ready to react to specific food allergens in the future.

The next time that person eats a food he or she is allergic to, the body reacts very quickly. The allergens move to mast cells and interact with the corresponding IgE on the mast cell's surface. In turn, the mast cells release certain chemicals such as histamine that help combat illnesses. However, if the individual has too much histamine in the blood, for example, that person will feel sick. Because there are no harmful viruses or

It's often easy to confuse a food allergy with a food intolerance. Although symptoms can be unpleasant, having an intolerance to a food is a less serious condition than having a food allergy and does not involve the immune system. Determining whether you have a food allergy or food intolerance is essential because the possible results of a mistaken diagnosis can be serious or even dangerous. People who have true allergies to foods need to know which foods to avoid, how to recognize the symptoms of an allergic attack, and how to take steps to prevent or handle a severe allergic reaction.

FOOD ALLERGY OR FOOD INTOLERANCE?

bacteria to fight, histamine instead causes an allergic reaction, such as rashes, hives, itching, and other symptoms. Mast cells also produce another type of chemical that makes an allergic reaction last longer by signaling other cells to move to the allergen and destroy it.

WHEN SYMPTOMS ARE NOT FOOD ALLERGIES

Sometimes people believe they have a food allergy if they do not like bananas or have physical reactions after eating peppers, onions, or other foods. For instance, they may experience stomach cramps, bloating, diarrhea, gas, or other digestive problems. Although these symptoms mimic a food allergy, another food-induced problem could be the cause, such as an intolerance to a certain

Some people avoid all dairy foods, including ice cream, because they have digestive problems after eating milk products. However, their discomfort could be due to a lactose intolerance.

food. In this case, the more someone eats of a particular food, the worse the symptoms become because the body does a poor job of digesting that food.

One of the most common intolerances is to lactose, a natural sugar found in milk and milk products, including ice cream, ice milk, sherbet, butter, and cheese. Individuals may not feel well when they eat a large amount of dairy foods in one meal. They can often avoid this discomfort by consuming small amounts of milk-based foods spread out during the day.

Celiac disease is not a true food allergy although it involves the immune

system. People with celiac disease are intolerant of gluten, a protein found in wheat, oats, rye, and barley. Eating gluten causes an immune response that damages the small intestine and prevents absorption of essential nutrients from some types of food. Symptoms of celiac disease include stomach pain, diarrhea, weight loss, and feeling tired.

COMMON SYMPTOMS

Most foods do not cause serious allergic reactions, although they may make someone feel sick for a few hours. Different people respond to the same allergen in different ways. They may be allergic to a specific food or a variety of foods. One individual might develop a mild rash from eating soy, while another could feel sick or experience stomach pain. The reactions depend on how allergic someone is to a particular food. Highly sensitive people can react to a food allergen just by touching or breathing it in, but this is extremely rare.

Many people instantly know when they are having a reaction after eating the wrong food, while others may have a delayed reaction of up to two hours. Typical symptoms usually occur in one or all of three major body systems: the skin, digestive, and respiratory systems. In severe reactions, the cardiovascular system (the heart and blood vessels, also known as the circulatory system) is involved.

During an allergic reaction, the most common part of the body affected is the skin. Mild to moderate itching, hives, and rashes may occur. Sometimes a dry, red,

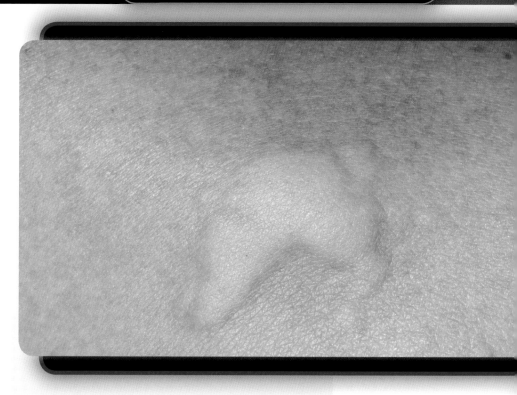

When a food allergy causes hives, the allergic reaction usually occurs immediately after eating the food, but it may emerge up to two hours later.

bumpy rash known as eczema flares up. The lips and eyelids may swell, causing them to become puffy and itch and burn. The eyes might also itch and turn red.

The digestive tract, which begins in the mouth and ends at the anus, may be affected next. Sometimes people say that they develop an odd, metallic taste in their mouth. Their tongue may swell, and they might have an itchy mouth, upset stomach, stomach pain, vomiting, or diarrhea. Although digestive symptoms can occur alone, they usually happen along with skin reactions.

A food allergy that affects the respiratory system can cause mild reactions, such as a runny or stuffy nose, sneezing, or slight coughing. More serious symptoms are swelling and tightening of the throat, wheezing, coughing, and shortness of breath. Individuals who have difficulty breathing may turn red and feel extremely sick. They might not feel well again until a day or two later.

RARE BUT DEADLY

Most allergic reactions are unpleasant but are not life-threatening. However, a severe reaction, known as anaphylaxis, can occur. Symptoms develop very quickly and affect the entire body. Many people feel a sense of doom or looming trouble just before their symptoms begin. Suddenly, they may experience severe itching of the eyes or face and the eruption of hives and itching across the entire body. It is also possible to have anaphylaxis without any rash or itching emerging.

Within minutes, more serious symptoms appear, such as stomach cramps, vomiting, and diarrhea. The throat and airways may swell, resulting in chest pain and difficulty swallowing, talking, or breathing. Other respiratory problems include wheezing, a whistling sound from the lungs when air goes in and out, and constant coughing.

If the heart and blood vessels are affected, the blood pressure drops. The heart rate slows and the kidneys may shut down. Individuals can become confused, weak, and, dizzy. They might turn pale or blue, collapse, and lose consciousness. Without immediate medical attention, death may result.

Although the risk of anaphylaxis is rare, it's very real. Everyone experiencing an anaphylactic reaction requires immediate medical help. According to FARE, severe food allergy reactions in the United States result in three hundred thousand emergency room visits each year, and more than two hundred deaths annually.

Anyone with a food allergy can potentially have an anaphylactic reaction. Most food anaphylaxis occurs from eating peanuts, tree nuts, fish, or shellfish. The risk of this reaction to a food allergen increases if you or a family member has asthma, eczema, or hay fever.

CHAPTER 2

WHO GETS A FOOD ALLERGY?

Food allergies are a serious health concern in the United States, and the number of people with food allergies is increasing. In 2013, the National Institute of Allergy and Infectious Diseases estimated that 5 percent of children under the age of five and 4 percent of teens and adults have a food allergy. Many scientists think the development of food allergies is influenced by both genetic and environmental factors.

LOOKING AT FAMILIES

Genes passed on to you from your parents determine various physical characteristics, such as your height, hair color, skin color, and nose shape. Food allergies may also be inherited because they often occur in families. Children have a greater chance of developing a food allergy if one or both parents have a food allergy. However, children in the family might not have the same allergy as their parents.

Parents who have allergies frequently pass along the tendency to have these conditions to their children. If the parents in a family do not have allergies, their children have a low chance of developing one. The likelihood of developing an allergy increases if one parent is affected by an allergy. The odds jump even higher if both parents have an allergy.

Many different genes control the manufacturing of IgE by the immune system. By studying genetics and learning how different genes work, researchers hope to discover why parents or siblings in the same family can have different food allergies. For example, a sibling may be allergic to peanuts and tree nuts, while another sibling reacts only to dairy products.

Scientists do know that specific allergy proteins and symptoms of allergies vary among family members. A parent who is allergic to salmon may have a mild reaction after consuming the fish. A teen in the family might have an anaphylactic reaction when eating salmon for the first time. Allergies, though, are not contagious. They cannot spread from person to person like a cold or flu virus.

FOOD ALLERGIES AND AGE

Anyone can develop a food allergy at any age. The condition is more common in children, particularly in the first years of life. Infants and babies are at higher risk than other age groups because their immune system and digestive system are not yet fully developed. For this reason, irritating foods may more easily pass into their bloodstream, increasing the likelihood of an allergic response from the immune system. These food allergies can disappear as their immune system gradually stops reacting to an allergen. However, not all children outgrow their allergies. In addition, teens and adults might develop new allergies to a food that they once could eat without any problem.

Exploring Environmental Theories

In addition to genetics, scientists are investigating environmental factors that may explain the increase in people having food allergies. One idea is the hygiene theory, which says that persons living in overly clean surroundings are more likely to develop allergies. Concerns about cleanliness may have an impact on the increase of allergies. Families today use a variety of different products for their dishes, countertops, sinks, ovens, bathtubs, showers, windows, carpets, floors, and clothes. They clean themselves with disinfectant soaps and shampoos. Because the chemicals in these items destroy numerous bacteria that could cause illness, children are not exposed to many common germs. Their immune system may instead attack harmless substances, such as peanuts, tree nuts, or shellfish.

The hygiene theory suggests that the overly clean state of people and their homes is upsetting the normal development of the immune system, causing more allergic tendencies.

According to the hygiene theory, children exposed to high levels of bacteria may be protected against developing allergies. Some researchers have found that children who grow up on farms, attend daycare, or have more than one sibling seem to have fewer allergies. Having less contact with a variety of bacteria may explain why allergic diseases are more widespread in urban areas than rural areas. It also might account for the increase of allergies in many areas as overall cleanliness has improved.

The rise in food allergies may be caused by other environmental factors, such as the food individuals eat. Since the 1960s, fresh, homemade meals have made up a smaller and smaller proportion of what people eat. Today, most individuals consume a broad range of processed foods, such as ready-made meals, snacks, and sweets at home, in restaurants, or on the go. Processing is anything that changes a food from the form it is in at the time of harvest. Additives are often added to an enormous number of processed foods, including crackers, breads, cereals, snacks, cookies, deli meats, and frozen or boxed meals such as pizza. These chemicals help food stay fresh longer and add color, flavor, and scent. Whether the additives in processed foods are causing an increase in food allergies is not yet known.

Another possible influence on the rise of food allergies is a growing awareness of the issue, which is encouraging individuals to be tested and diagnosed. Allergists also have ready access to reliable allergy tests. These two factors could mean that the number of people with food allergies has not actually changed, but doctors are better

Some people are concerned that genetically modified foods, like these tomatoes, may create new food allergies because the imported genes might produce a novel protein that triggers allergic reactions.

at diagnosing the condition. However, it's unlikely that these aspects alone can explain the climb in the number of young people with food allergies.

Some people believe that foods modified by biotechnology, also known as genetically modified organisms (GMOs), are contributing to the increase in food allergies. Scientists have used gene technology to improve the yield of dozens of food plants, including corn, soybeans, tomatoes, cantaloupe, papaya, and sugar beets (a source of table sugar). Not all of these products are yet available

Individuals with pollen-related allergy syndrome can often inactivate the allergens by cooking the problematic fruits and vegetables. However, stir-fried and other lightly cooked vegetables may still cause a reaction.

in supermarkets in the United States. Today's GMOs do not contain proteins from known allergic foods. It's possible, though, that introducing a gene into a plant can create a new allergen or cause an allergic reaction in some individuals. Food manufacturers may voluntarily label whether their foods have been developed through genetic engineering.

SPOTTING OTHER FOOD ALLERGIES

A common food allergy in adults is to specific raw fruits and vegetables. This condition is known as oral allergy syndrome or pollen-related allergy syndrome. The lips, mouth, or tongue may tingle, swell, or itch slightly after eating apples, pears, peaches, melons, cherries, celery, or carrots, for example. The symptoms occur because of reactions with certain pollens that closely resemble food proteins. Individuals with an allergy to tree pollens might have an itchy mouth when eating apples, cherries, or peaches, while those with a ragweed allergy may react to carrots or melons.

Sometimes people can eat cooked apples, carrots, celery, or other fruits and vegetables

without any reactions because heat breaks down the pollen proteins, and the immune system does not fire up. Peeling fruit or dipping it into lemon juice may also be helpful. Oral allergy syndrome usually develops in older children, teens, and young adults. It can also appear later in life.

Individuals with a food allergy may have severe allergic reactions if they jog, bicycle, play tennis, dance, or participate in other vigorous activities after eating a particular food. Researchers do not know why this reaction happens. One theory is that the blood vessels change during heavy exercising, triggering allergy symptoms that may result in exercise-induced anaphylaxis. During this serious reaction, people might experience a pounding headache, dizziness, wheezing, chest pain, and vomiting. They could collapse and even die if they are not treated for anaphylaxis right away. Fortunately, exercise-induced anaphylaxis is exceedingly rare.

CHAPTER 3

Different people are allergic to different foods. A teen, for example, may be allergic to only one food, while another young person might have multiple food allergies. All food allergens have something in common—they are made up of large, complex proteins. The most common allergies for children are milk, eggs, peanuts, soy, tree nuts, and wheat. In adults, the list includes fish, shellfish, tree nuts, and peanuts.

MILK AND ITS MANY PRODUCTS

Cow's milk is the most common food allergy in young children in the United States. Symptoms are usually mild, and most kids outgrow the allergy by age three or four. However, a small number of people remain allergic to milk and other dairy foods as teens and adults.

Two proteins in cow's milk, casein and whey, trigger most allergic reactions. Cheese, butter, yogurt, cream, half-and-half, puddings, and ice cream are all dairy foods. Manufacturers add milk and milk proteins to a wide array of foods, including margarine, lunch meats, cakes, cookies, breads, chips, crackers, cereals, and some candies. Milk proteins can show up in

The main culprit in a milk allergy is cow's milk, but milk from sheep, goats, and buffalo can also cause an allergic reaction.

unlikely products, such as sherbet, canned tuna, artificial butter flavor, chewing gum, and soy cheeses. Milk proteins are sometimes simply called casein, caseinate, or whey. Many nondairy foods contain these proteins, which are added during the products' manufacturing.

THE WHITE AND YELLOW OF EGGS

Like milk allergy, egg allergy is most common in young children, but is usually outgrown before the teen years. Most people actually react to the proteins in the egg white. Because it's difficult to separate the white and yolk, allergists recommend avoiding eggs and any products made with them. Product labels that list albumin, globulin, lecithin, mayonnaise, meringue, or ovalbumin signal the use of eggs in the products. Eggs are usually an ingredient in baked goods, cereals, ice

Sometimes nonfood items contain eggs, such as cosmetics, shampoos, and medications. People who are very sensitive to egg proteins should check with the manufacturer before using these products.

cream, marshmallows, salad dressings, pastas, soups, meatloaf and other processed meats, and some candies.

A very small number of medications contain egg. Egg protein is part of the measles, mumps, and rubella (MMR) vaccine, but medical experts agree that the vaccine is safe for children who have an egg allergy. Although the annual influenza, or flu, vaccine may have a trace amount of egg, it can be given to most people

FOOD ALLERGENS, LABELING, AND THE LAW

The Food Allergen Labeling and Consumer Protection Act (FALCPA) requires manufacturers to clearly identify any of these eight major allergens in packaged foods: milk, peanuts, tree nuts, eggs, soy, wheat, shellfish, and fish. Companies must display the food allergen in the ingredient list, such as "tree nut (almond)" or "whey (milk)." Or, the ingredients list may have a separate line stating "Contains," followed by the name of the allergen. An example is "Contains soy." The law also covers additives, spice blends, colorings, and flavorings with allergens. For instance, a label might state "natural flavors (walnut, peanut)." If you have a food allergy, you should be careful about eating a food whose label says "may contain," "manufactured in a facility," "made on equipment with," or "free from allergens," because these voluntary labels are not covered by law and may or may not reflect the actual presence of an allergen. The U.S. Food and Drug Administration (FDA) is working to make food labels easier to read and understand.

without any complications. A flu vaccine without egg is available for anyone older than eighteen. Teens should talk to their doctor about any concerns they might have about getting these vaccines.

No Peanuts Forever?

Peanut allergy has gained public attention because allergic reactions to peanuts may be severe for some people. Eating even a tiny piece of peanut can trigger a dangerous chain of events, leading to life-threatening anaphylaxis. Direct skin contact might also produce adverse symptoms in highly allergic individuals. According to FARE, peanut allergies make up about half of the emergency room visits and deaths caused by all food allergies every year.

Peanut allergy is diagnosed most frequently in babies and young children. Only about 20 percent, or two out of every ten children, outgrow this allergy. Peanuts are not related to tree nuts, such as almonds, pecans, cashews, or walnuts. Instead, they are a vegetable and grow in the soil. They belong to the legume family, which is made up of peas and beans.

As with milk and eggs, peanuts are regularly used in a huge variety of manufactured foods. Besides peanut butter, they frequently appear in mixed nuts, trail mixes, baked goods, ice cream, cereals, energy bars, and candy. They may be added to salad dressings, sauces, and chili. Even if peanuts are not in the ingredient list, it's a good idea to be on the alert for messages on food labels like "Produced in a facility that uses peanuts," "May contain peanuts," and "Traces of peanuts."

CRACKING NUTS: THE INSIDE STORY

Nuts are hard-shelled dry fruits that have an edible inside kernel, or seed, and grow on trees. (The word "nut" is also used to refer to the edible kernel.) A tree nut allergy can develop at any age and tends to last a lifetime. The first reaction, though, usually occurs in children and teens. Many kinds of nuts are popular in the United States, including walnuts, almonds, pecans, cashews, pine nuts, pistachios, Brazil nuts, and macadamias. People may be allergic to one nut, some nuts, or all of them. Unfortunately, once you have an allergic reaction to one tree nut, you have a good chance of reacting to another type of nut.

The proteins of tree nuts and peanuts share some common characteristics. For this reason, even if you are allergic to only tree nuts or peanuts, your allergist may recommend avoiding both foods. Like peanuts, tree nuts can cause severe effects. Even if someone with a nut allergy eats just a tiny piece, anaphylactic reactions can occur. Nuts are usually found in many of the same foods as peanuts, making it challenging to avoid eating them.

THE PROBLEM WITH SOY

Soy allergy is diagnosed most often in infants. Children usually outgrow this allergy, but some remain allergic to soy for life. Soybeans belong to the legume family, along with peanuts and peas. Reactions are usually unpleasant, but not serious. Interestingly, most people with a peanut allergy are not allergic to soy.

You may be surprised about how many food labels say "Contains soy." It's a staple in cereals, soups, meat products, sauces, salad dressings, butter and meat substitutes, energy bars, candies, ice cream, and baked goods. Herbal supplements sometimes contain soy.

Wheat allergy is caused by an allergic reaction to one or more of the proteins found in wheat: albumin, globulin, gluten, and gliadin. Most reactions involve albumin and globulin.

Tofu, soy milk, edamame, miso, soy sauce, and tamari are popular soy foods. You may see many other names for this bean, including soya, soybeans, soy protein, hydrolyzed vegetable protein, textured vegetable protein (TVP), lecithin, monodiglyceride, monosodium glutamate (MSG), and vitamin E.

SCOUTING FOR WHEAT

Most people with a wheat allergy react to gluten, a group of proteins contained in foods that are processed from wheat, rye, barley, and oats. Wheat is the most common base for flour. That makes gluten a very difficult food allergen to avoid because pasta, breads, cakes, cookies, pies, breakfast cereals, energy bars, and many other foods contain wheat flour. It's in soups, spice mixes, salad dressings, soy and other sauces, frozen and boxed food, processed meats, ketchup, and candy. This grain is even part of some cheese, yogurt, ice cream, and other milk products. Other unusual items that may have gluten are canned chipotle peppers, canned tuna, imitation bacon, imitation seafood, root beer, and herbal supplements. You always must be on your guard while scouting for gluten-free products.

A wheat allergy in children is usually seen in infants or young children and is typically outgrown by age five. Teens and adults seldom develop this allergy. Most people with a wheat allergy can safely eat barley, rye, oats, and other grains. However, it's important to ask your allergist what grains are safe for you to consume.

SHELLFISH AND FISH FRENZY

Shellfish and fish allergies can occur in children but usually first develop in teens and adults and typically last a lifetime. There are two distinct groups of shellfish:

Pro football player Adrian Peterson, diagnosed with seafood allergies as an adult, helped launch an educational program called Ready2Go for people with food and other allergies.

crustaceans (including shrimp, crab, and lobster) and mollusks (such as clams, mussels, oysters, scallops, octopuses, and squid). Common shellfish allergies include shrimp, lobster, and crab. A well-known instance of a newly developed shellfish allergy occurred to Adrian Peterson, the star running back for the Minnesota Vikings football team and the National Football League's most valuable player in 2012. In July 2012, soon after eating a favorite meal of seafood gumbo, he began having severe allergic reactions. Luckily, Peterson was rushed to a hospital emergency room for immediate treatment of anaphylaxis, which saved his life. Tests showed that he had developed allergies to shrimp, scallops, and lobster. To be safe, doctors recommend that anyone allergic to one kind of shellfish avoid all types of shellfish.

People can be allergic to only one kind of fish, such as salmon, cod, tuna, or catfish. More than half of the time, though, they have an allergy to all fish. Fish and shellfish do not come from related food families. Being allergic to either fish or shellfish may not mean that you must avoid both. Everyone should first check with his or her allergist.

Shellfish and fish allergies might cause mild reactions, such as hives or itching, or severe responses that could be life-threatening. If someone is highly allergic to these foods, eating even a tiny amount can trigger serious reactions. Sometimes fish or shellfish are hidden ingredients in soups, sauces, dressings, and artificial seafood.

CHAPTER 4

FINDING THE
FORBIDDEN FOODS

The best way for teens to find out whether they have a food allergy is to see an allergist. These doctors are experts in diagnosing and treating allergies and can help you learn how to manage your condition. Allergists use various tests to correctly diagnosis food allergies. You should not try to test yourself because you could become very ill. Allergists may also ask teens to keep a food diary of all foods and beverages they consume over a period of time.

MEDICAL HISTORIES AND PHYSICAL EXAMS

Diagnosing food allergies involves several steps, and these steps take time, patience, and careful work by teens and their parents and allergist. A key piece of a correct diagnosis is documenting someone's medical and family history. To begin, allergists ask individuals to describe the problematic food and their symptoms after eating it, and when these reactions start and stop. People with severe allergies usually have reactions within thirty to sixty minutes after eating the allergen, but delayed symptoms can also occur. Information about allergies that you and other family members may have is also important information to give to the allergist.

When taking a medical history, allergists want to know about the person's health in the past. They will also ask about someone's lifestyle, home life, and diet.

Next, these doctors perform a physical exam. They listen to a teen's breathing. The skin, chest, eyes, ears, nose, and throat are examined for any signs of infection. If a food allergy is suspected, allergists conduct tests to find what foods may be causing the problem.

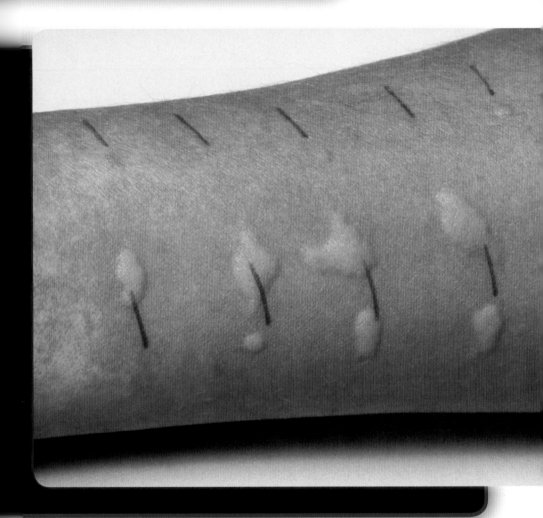

SEARCHING FOR ALLERGIES WITH SKIN AND BLOOD TESTS

Allergists can order several different types of tests to determine if someone has a food allergy. The two basic kinds are skin tests and blood tests. Skin tests are extremely sensitive and help determine which allergen

This teen has some positive skin tests to specific allergens. The allergist may require other tests to confirm that the individual has one or more food allergies.

triggers reactions in people who have a food allergy. They are the most common method of allergy testing. These tests are inexpensive, with minor itching as the main effect, and can be used for all ages.

Allergists use a small, plastic device to scratch or prick the skin with a tiny drop of an extract from a food, usually on the arm or back. Extracts from different foods can be tested at the same time in rows of separate scratches or pricks. A raised, red bump that looks like a mosquito bite may form on the skin within fifteen to twenty minutes. If that happens, the test is positive, indicating that the individual might have a food allergy. Any redness usually fades within an hour after the testing. If no reaction occurs, someone is not likely to have an allergy to the specific food.

Because a skin test could trigger anaphylaxis, allergists may use a radioallergosorbent (RAST) test for anyone who appears to be severely allergic to a food. A RAST test measures the amount of specific IgE antibodies in the blood. For this test, a health professional draws a small amount of blood from the arm and sends it to a medical laboratory for processing. A positive RAST test result indicates a high number of IgE antibodies in the blood, signifying that an individual may have a food allergy.

Blood tests are more expensive and less reliable than skin tests but are necessary for people who are at risk of severe allergic reactions. They are also used if individuals have a skin condition, such as eczema, or are taking certain medicines.

THE QUEST FOR ALLERGENS CONTINUES

Allergists may ask people with a suspected allergy to keep a food diary for several weeks. During that time, teens record everything they eat and drink, any symptoms, and when the symptoms appeared. Food diaries cannot prove that a particular food causes specific symptoms, but they can show possible links between certain foods and symptoms.

You can set up a food diary on a worksheet in a word processing or spreadsheet program. Or, use a notebook or sheets of paper clipped together. Enter the title "Food Diary" and the dates of the week, such as December 8–14. Then, make a table with several columns to write

Just a few weeks of record keeping, including what you eat and how you feel in the hours that follow, can reveal useful information to your allergist.

down the date, time, food or beverage you ate and drank, and any symptoms. Here is an example of a food diary that you can create to record what's consumed each day of the week:

Food Diary, December 8–14

Day	Time	Food	Time Symptoms Began	Symptoms
Sunday	7:00 AM	2 waffles, butter, maple syrup, orange juice	7:45 AM	mild headache
	10:30 AM	apple, peanut butter on crackers	11:00 AM	rash
	12:30 PM	hamburger on bun, ketchup, french fries		
	3:00 PM	smoothie with milk	3:15 PM	coughing
	5:45 PM	salmon, salad with dressing, potato, sour cream, butter	6:00 PM	tongue swelling
	8:00 PM	banana, popcorn		
Monday	6:00 AM	2 peanut butter granola bars, energy drink	6:25 AM	itchy skin
	11:30 AM	Spaghetti and meatballs, milk, applesauce	12:10 PM	coughing
	3:00 PM	energy drink, salt water taffy		
	5:30 PM	fried chicken, corn, green beans, bread, butter, ice cream	6:00 PM	vomiting
Tuesday etc.				

Two easy-to-use apps for smartphones and tablets are Allergy Journal and mySymptoms. Both apps allow you to save or e-mail reports to your allergist. Some people use Google Calendar, iCalendar Yahoo, or another online calendar to track their daily food and drink intake and any symptoms that may occur.

An elimination diet may help uncover a food allergy. For this test, your allergist will ask you to completely avoid a suspicious food for several weeks. If your symptoms improve, the food is added to your diet and you are carefully checked for reactions. This process is repeated for every suspected food allergen. Conducting an elimination diet can take four to six weeks or longer.

Allergists may decide to perform a food challenge to see whether a food causes symptoms when eaten. During this test, an individual is given gradually increasing amounts of a suspect food, while a doctor watches for reactions. The test is stopped at the first sign of symptoms. Food challenges should always be carried out where medical care is immediately available because medications may be needed to treat an anaphylactic reaction.

Unmasking Phony Tests

Various websites on the Internet promise easy methods to diagnose and cure food allergies. Some of these techniques include hair analysis, applied kinesiology, resistance testing, and pulse testing. However, these

FINDING A KNOWLEDGEABLE ALLERGIST

If you have symptoms of a possible food allergy, it's best not to self-diagnose. Instead, see a certified allergist who can provide an accurate diagnosis. These doctors have specialized training on allergies, must take ongoing medical classes, and also pass a certification test regularly. A list of certified allergists is available on the website of the American Board of Allergy and Immunology (ABAI). Your primary care doctor can also refer you to an allergist, or you can ask relatives or friends for recommendations. Most health insurance companies provide a list of participating allergists on their websites, so you can also check allergist names there. In addition, the American Academy of Allergy, Asthma, and Immunology (AAAAI) website provides a list of allergists by zip code. It's a good idea to write down any of your symptoms, medications, and questions and bring this information with you to the appointment. A good allergist will carefully answer questions and concerns to help you understand your food allergy and how best to take care of yourself.

tests are not medically proven or reliable. Allergists and other doctors do not use them for their diagnoses. In addition, these questionable methods are usually costly and might stop people from getting effective treatment for a true food allergy.

Analyzing hair involves studying the mineral content of hair. Advertisers claim that this analysis can show whether someone lacks certain minerals that are causing the food allergy. Minerals in hair, though, have no connection with food allergies.

Applied kinesiology is a method to determine muscle strength after foods or other items are placed in the mouth or put into a glass bottle and held in the hand. Any muscle weakness supposedly shows that someone has a food allergy. This technique has no medical basis and is an inaccurate way to evaluate a food allergy.

In resistance testing, also known as vega testing or electrodermal testing, electronic equipment measures the electricity that flows through the body. At the same time, an individual holds food in the hand or on an aluminum plate. A computer generates the results of the test. As with hair analysis and applied kinesiology, resistance tests are useless for detecting a food allergy.

The pulse test says that if people are allergic to certain foods, their pulse rate, or heartbeat, will rise after eating those foods. There is no connection between food and pulse rate. In fact, someone's heartbeat can go up over a concern about taking this test!

New, undependable tests turn up regularly. If you see or hear about a food allergy test or treatment that seems interesting, ask your doctor about it. FARE publishes an up-to-date list of unproven diagnostic tests on its website.

MYTH

An individual with a food allergy always has the same symptoms of an allergic reaction.

FACT

Individuals may experience the same, less, or more severe symptoms than what they encountered in the past. Someone might have a rash with one reaction, and hives and stomach pain with a later reaction.

MYTH

Home test kits can be used to diagnosis food allergies.

FACT

Health professionals do not recommend these tests because they are usually poor in quality and are unreliable indicators of a food allergy. In addition, these home tests can create harmful risks.

MYTH

Anyone can be allergic to food additives, such as food colorings, sulfites, nitrates, butylated hydroxyanisole (BHA), high fructose corn syrup, inulin, or sodium benzoate.

FACT

A wide variety of food additives can cause mild to severe chemical reactions in some individuals. These reactions are known as food or chemical sensitivities because the immune system is not involved.

CHAPTER 5

MANAGING REACTIONS

Once an allergy is diagnosed, the only proven way to manage it is to avoid the foods that cause problems. That's not always easy to do. If an allergic reaction does occur, people can take medicines to make their symptoms milder and easier to handle. They must also be ready to treat a severe allergic reaction with an injection of epinephrine, a synthetic form of the hormone adrenaline. Quick medical treatment with this drug can save lives. There is no cure for food allergies yet, but scientists are working to make them easier to live with and less life-threatening.

MILD AND STRONGER REACTIONS

A very mild allergic reaction to a food allergen may not require any medicine. Symptoms can be in a small area of the body, such as a faint rash on the face or arm. After a while, the symptoms disappear and the individual feels better.

A variety of medications are available to help people manage stronger—but not severe—reactions. Over-the-counter (nonprescription) drugs work for some individuals, while others may need prescription drugs. Everyone who has a food allergy should talk with his or her allergist before using a particular medicine. Pharmacists also can provide information about over-the-counter and prescription drugs.

Common drugs used to relieve allergy symptoms include antihistamines. More than a dozen are available with or without a doctor's prescription. These medicines reduce the effect of histamine, the main chemical that causes allergic reactions. Antihistamines work quickly to stop itching, a runny nose, and sneezing. They come as pills, tablets, or liquids. If one type of antihistamine does not work for you, try another one.

Doctors may prescribe glucocorticoids, usually known as steroids, for people with breathing difficulties. These powerful drugs decrease inflammation, or swelling, in the airways and ease breathing. They must be used regularly to be effective and are especially helpful for people with asthma and severe allergies.

HANDLING ANAPHYLAXIS

People with food allergies should always be prepared for anaphylaxis. They need to know the warning signs and have their medications immediately available. Anaphylactic shock is frightening to the individual having the attack and also for anyone watching the occurrence. Knowing what to do can help ease everyone's fears and help save lives. The sooner anaphylaxis is treated, the greater the chance of survival. In addition, if a young person has had anaphylaxis before,

Anyone with a food allergy must know how to use an autoinjector correctly and quickly. Here are the six steps for using the commonly prescribed EpiPen®:

1. Form a fist around the EpiPen® with one hand, pointing the orange tip down. The tip contains the needle.
2. Pull off the blue safety release cap with the other hand.
3. Place the orange tip against the outer thigh, with or without clothes. Do not touch the tip with your fingers.
4. Quickly push down hard until a click is heard or felt and hold the EpiPen® in place for ten seconds. The dose of epinephrine is released.
5. Remove the EpiPen®. An orange safety shield now covers the needle.
6. Get to an emergency room immediately. Take the EpiPen® to show the doctor and ask for proper disposal.

BLUE UP, ORANGE DOWN

it's more likely to happen when exposed to the same allergen again.

Severe reactions can develop within minutes after eating a problem food. Sometimes mild symptoms progress into serious reactions over the course of an hour or two. If anaphylactic reactions begin, the throat closes up, the pulse drops, and breathing becomes difficult. The individual then requires immediate treatment with epinephrine to help reverse these severe reactions. Although an antihistamine relieves the discomfort of

1 Pull off grey safety release.

Retirez le dispositif de sécurité gris.

2 Push black tip firmly into outer thigh so it 'clicks' AND HOLD on thigh for several seconds.

Planter l'embout noir sur la partie externe de la cuisse jusqu'au déclic ET MAINTENIR en place pendant quelques secondes.

Seek medical attention.

Obtenir des soins médicaux.

itching, hives, or other skin reactions, it does not help with anaphylaxis.

The first-line drug for anaphylaxis is epinephrine, which is injected into the muscle of the outer thigh with an autoinjector. These small, pencil-shaped tubes are prescribed by doctors. Autoinjectors contain a combined syringe and a small, hidden needle. The syringe holds one dose of epinephrine and can be used only once. People say that the injection feels like a pinch, but it's not painful. A variety of autoinjectors are available, including EpiPen®, Adrenaclick®, and Auvi-Q®. It's essential to have a doctor, allergist, or another health professional show anyone with an allergy how to use an autoinjector because each device is a little different. Parents and guardians of minors with allergies should also know how to administer epinephrine shots.

Epinephrine quickly moves through the body, helping to prevent anaphylactic shock. It reverses throat swelling, relaxes the lungs to improve breathing, and stimulates the heartbeat. The drug is effective for ten to fifteen minutes, usually enough time for an emergency team to arrive and get an individual to a hospital for further treatment. Going to a hospital is critical because someone's problems can suddenly get worse. Or, a person may seem recovered, but a second wave of symptoms can occur a few hours later. For this reason, it's important to be in a hospital where the

Autoinjectors are easy to use and have saved many lives. They immediately get epinephrine into the bloodstream, which is then rapidly carried throughout the body, helping to avert life-threatening anaphylaxis.

To remain vigilant in case of a potential emergency, people with known food allergies must carry their two autoinjectors and antihistamines at all times.

individual can be closely monitored after having an anaphylactic attack for four or more hours.

Being Prepared for Severe Reactions

Doctors advise people with a food allergy to carry antihistamines and two autoinjectors on them at all times. To reach their medicine quickly, teens can place the items in a pocket, purse, backpack, or shoulder pouch, or clipped on a belt. Usually no one will question you about what you are carrying.

It's best to store autoinjectors in their carrier tubes at room temperature, between 59°F to 86°F (15°C to 30°C)—not in the refrigerator or car. To make

sure the medication is safe and effective for use during an emergency, everyone should check their autoinjectors regularly and replace them when they expire. Some people practice injections by using expired devices on an orange. They can also ask their doctor for a training device that does not have a needle. Family members and friends need to know how to use an autoinjector in the event of an emergency.

Allergists strongly recommend wearing a medical emergency necklace, pendant, bracelet, sports band, shoe tag, or watch that describes your allergy. Several companies make them and offer a variety of styles. You may want to list your food allergies and "anaphylaxis," such as "peanut anaphylaxis," or just "food allergy and anaphylaxis." The information on these devices tells emergency personnel and other people how to help when an attack begins or if someone is unconscious.

Hope for the Future

Scientists worldwide are studying many methods to reduce food allergy symptoms and prevent allergy attacks. For example, drug companies are developing antihistamines that work faster and have fewer unwanted effects, such as drowsiness. Another avenue of research is determining if parents can reduce the risk

When a life-threatening allergic attack occurs, the paramedics or medical emergency technicians can make immediate and proper treatment decisions if the individual is wearing medical emergency identification.

of their children developing food allergies by not feeding them certain foods early in life. Some experts are focused on learning how genes are involved in the creation of food allergies, while others are hoping to develop a vaccine for food allergies.

A promising treatment for food allergy is oral immunotherapy, in which small amounts of a food allergen are given to someone in increasing amounts over a period of time. The goal of this therapy is for the immune system to learn to accept the allergen without any symptoms. However, some people with food allergies may have severe reactions when trying this technique. To deal with this problem, scientists are giving individuals anti-IgE antibodies during oral immunotherapy. Researchers may find that combining both therapies will produce the best results for people with food allergies.

1. Given my food allergies, what are good ways for me to stay safe?

2. Can I eat foods that have "May contain" on the labels?

3. What medical treatments are available for my food allergy and which do you recommend?

4. Would you go over my emergency care plan with me?

5. How often should I be retested for my food allergy?

6. When I buy food, what should I watch out for on the labels?

7. Should my family and I ban my food allergens at home?

8. What are some safe food alternatives for me?

9. Do you have any good food allergy resources that you can recommend?

10. What lifestyle changes should I make to manage my food allergy?

10 GREAT QUESTIONS TO ASK AN ALLERGIST

CHAPTER 6

TAKING CONTROL

Having an existing or newly diagnosed food allergy impacts those teens who are affected in many ways. Because a food allergy is a chronic condition, they need to learn how to handle a great deal of responsibility for their own well-being. Young people must carefully watch what they eat and have medications and an emergency care plan available if severe reactions occur. Taking control of a food allergy means that the allergy does not interfere with a healthy, normal life.

SWIRLING EMOTIONS

People with an existing or new food allergy may react with a wide range of emotions, including anger, anxiety, and fear for their safety. They can feel sad, depressed, overwhelmed, and frustrated, or grieve over their restricted food choices. Some teens feel isolated and left out of social activities, such as celebrating a friend's birthday with

Learning to live with a food allergy can be difficult and may lead to sadness and despair. Teens can reach out and help friends who show signs of depression.

cake and ice cream. They may worry that family, friends, or other people see them as too fussy. Or, they might feel jealous of someone who has no issues with food. All of these emotions are normal and tend to come and go.

Having a food allergy can negatively affect someone's feelings. Many teens find they cope better by expressing their emotions when these occur. They may want to talk to a friend, family member, school counselor, or another trusted adult. Some young people work through unhappy feelings by journaling, blogging, painting, or drawing.

Like having asthma, diabetes, or other medical conditions, food allergies are a way of life. People who have a food allergy must understand, accept, and deal with their situation. Acceptance is essential to move forward and take control of their lives.

People who plan well often experience less stress when dealing with their food allergy. By deciding in advance what you need and want, you come into situations better prepared.

Family Adjustments

When you are newly diagnosed with a food allergy, you and your family require time to adjust to the effect of the diagnosis. Everyone must learn how to integrate your food limitations into their daily living and make necessary changes. For example, the family diet may need to be altered to accommodate the food allergy. The goal is for the family members to work together as a team to cope with your food allergy, which, if not treated, can be life threatening.

Teens who have food allergies may find it helpful to talk with their parents about common situations that could arise and brainstorm how to deal with different scenarios. For example, they can determine techniques to handle eating at a fast-food chain or restaurant with friends or going to a party where a variety of snacks will be available. Putting together a plan before an event can help young people avoid possible risks and allow them to relax and have fun.

Role-playing, or practicing different scenarios, with family members is also beneficial. Say you are shopping at the mall with friends. What would you do if everyone wants to split a pizza, but you are allergic to wheat or milk products, such as cheese? If you are at a party and have a severe allergic reaction, what steps should you take? Your family can help you learn to be prepared for everyday situations and emergencies.

TAKING ON MORE RESPONSIBILITY

Navigating through the teen years can be a challenging time for nearly everyone. It's a period of transition, from being a child to becoming an adult. Young people are learning to become independent and take on more responsibility in many aspects of their lives, including school, work, driving, dating, and health. They can become skilled at balancing a busy lifestyle while successfully managing their food allergy.

Everyone who has a food allergy must learn to take increased responsibility for his or her health. Individuals need to be in charge of their own actions, such as making safe and healthy choices about their diet at home, school, work, or elsewhere. They must become proficient at monitoring food allergens and avoiding them.

Teens can take control of their food allergy in other ways. For example, during office visits to their allergist, they may ask questions about medications and treatments. Being responsible means remembering to bring along two autoinjectors and antihistamines every time you leave the house. Young people can also talk to their parents about past mistakes to become more proactive in the future.

HOME ADVANTAGES

Having a family member with a food allergy means that the entire family must be aware of the condition

Teens can cook with allergy-friendly substitutes to make easy, everyday foods, including stir-fry, tacos, pizza, wraps, burgers, spaghetti, and pancakes. Cookies, brownies, and cupcakes may also be on the menu!

and take precautions at home. Depending on the severity of the allergy, the family may allow the allergen in the house or ban it entirely. It's important for everyone to agree on the rules and work together to follow them.

If it's acceptable to have food allergens at home, various strategies will help keep the particular person who has a food allergy safe. One method is to store clearly marked foods separately in the refrigerator, cupboard, or pantry. To keep allergens from spreading throughout the house, families can set rules as to where foods can be eaten, such as only in the kitchen and dining room.

Cooking at home allows you to control what is in your

CONTAINING CROSS-CONTAMINATION

Always take precautions against cross-contamination, which occurs when a safe food comes into contact with an allergen during food preparation, cooking, eating, or serving. To keep this contamination from happening, families can designate allergen-free food preparation areas, kitchen tools, pots, pans, dishes, forks, and so on. It's critical to thoroughly clean all cutting boards, tables, and other surfaces that have touched food allergens. Some families use colored plastic cutting boards to avoid confusion. Family members should wash their hands before preparing meals, before serving food, and after meals.

snacks and meals. When you cook or bake from scratch, you can usually find substitutes for ingredients you must avoid, such as rice or quinoa flour for wheat flour or pumpkin or sunflower seeds for nuts. Supermarkets offer an amazing variety of foods that are free from peanuts, tree nuts, milk, egg, wheat, soy, and other common allergens. Books, magazines, the Internet, and social networking sites such as Facebook provide a wealth of allergy-free recipes for new and experienced cooks and bakers.

THE LOWDOWN ON LABELS

To stay safe, people with food allergies must check all food labels. The Food Allergen Labeling and Consumer Protection Act (FALCPA) requires allergen labeling of packaged foods sold in the United States. By law, the top

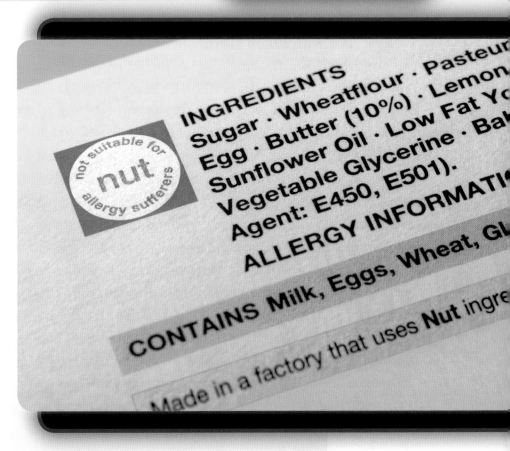

The federal government does not require companies to disclose whether a product could be cross-contaminated with any of the eight major food allergens during the manufacturing process.

eight food allergens—milk, egg, fish, shellfish, tree nuts, wheat, peanuts, and soy—must be listed on the product label. The specific types of tree nuts, fish, and shellfish also need to be stated on the label, as well as the major food allergens in spices, flavorings, additives, and colorings.

Everyone with a food allergy should check the labels on nonprescription medications, oral care products, and cosmetics like lipstick and lip balm. Such products may contain allergens such as milk, egg, wheat, or nuts. The FALCPA does not cover these items.

It's critical to read the list of ingredients in food products every time you buy them. Sometimes manufacturers change the ingredients of foods without warning. In addition, the same food from individual manufacturers is frequently prepared differently.

If there is any doubt about a product's ingredients, teens should not buy or eat the item. Instead, they can ask their doctor or allergist or a registered dietitian about any foods they might question. A physician can recommend a registered dietitian or people can set up their own appointment. Dietitians provide information on allergen-safe cooking, grocery shopping, reading food labels, eating at restaurants, and identifying hidden allergens. Another option is to contact the food manufacturer and ask questions about the food. The product label usually contains the company name, address, telephone number, and website.

MAKING AN ALLERGY EMERGENCY KIT

No matter how diligent teens or others are about watching what they eat, they could consume a tiny piece of an unsafe food and trigger an allergic reaction.

That's why they should have an emergency plan. This strategy includes keeping an allergy emergency kit in a safe, convenient location. You can make an emergency kit by putting the following items in a case, bag, backpack, or other container:

- Your medications, including an antihistamine and two epinephrine autoinjectors
- Your food allergy emergency care plan

Allergy emergency care plans are written instructions describing what to do if someone has an allergic reaction. A plan includes the name of the individual, allergies, mild and severe symptoms and treatment to provide if they occur, and contact information. An allergist usually writes a plan for anyone under the age of eighteen. You can also get a form from your doctor, school, or the website of the American Academy of Allergy, Asthma, and Immunology; American College of Allergy, Asthma, and Immunology; Asthma and Allergy Foundation of America; and Food Allergy Research & Education.

Teens should regularly go over their emergency plan with their allergist. They can post their plan in a common space at home, such as on the refrigerator, family bulletin board, or bathroom cabinet. Everyone in your home should know what to do if you have an allergic reaction to food.

CHAPTER 7

YOUR SOCIAL LIFE

Teens who live with a food allergy have their social life affected, including their interactions with friends, dates, classmates, teachers, and other people. Although food limitations are an ongoing concern, eating can still be fun and enjoyable for them. Teens who accept their food allergy as part of their lives learn to take care of themselves in a variety of situations.

SUPPORTIVE FRIENDS

Some young people may not want others to know about their food allergy, especially if they are newly diagnosed.

A close friend is more likely to share with you what he or she is actually feeling and thinking. This can also make you feel comfortable talking about your food allergy.

They may need time to work through the many changes in their life or are too embarrassed to tell anyone. However, it's important to tell family and friends. Not everyone needs to be told, but you should let your closest friends know about it.

Keeping a food allergy a secret is stressful. It means hiding your medications when you are with friends or making excuses about why you cannot eat what everyone else is having. It's distressing to pretend that everything is fine when you feel ill after eating a food allergen or have severe reactions that clearly require medical attention. Not using appropriate medications or not getting immediate help is potentially life-threatening.

When friends are first told about your food allergy, they might ask questions. That curiosity is a common response. You can explain the foods you need to avoid, how to recognize the symptoms of a reaction, and what to do in an emergency. Describing the basic facts can take just a few minutes, unless friends want to know more. FARE offers a peer education program called Be a PAL (Protect a Life from Food Allergies). It helps teens teach their friends about avoiding food allergens and what to do if reactions occur.

The more friends understand about your food allergy, the more they can support you. For instance, they may want to assist by checking food labels or asking a restaurant server about particular menu items. Perhaps they may stop you from eating something that could contain a food allergen. Friends can provide tremendous support and help you manage your food allergy in potentially risky situations. However, it is always up to you to stay alert for problems and take any necessary steps to protect yourself.

THE DOUBLE HARM OF BULLYING

Young people may be teased or bullied about their food allergy. For example, someone might try to trick them into eating peanuts, eggs, tree nuts, soy, or other foods that can trigger a reaction. Some teens with a serious peanut allergy have had peanuts put into their school locker or peanut butter smeared on their forehead. These actions can put their lives in danger, which is extremely scary and upsetting. On top of that, they now carry a double load: worrying about what they eat and watching if someone is trying to harm them because of their condition.

Individuals who are harassed may feel embarrassed, sad, fearful, anxious, helpless, or angry. If bullying continues, people can become depressed and withdrawn at home and school and in the community. They may find it challenging to talk about their true feelings and have difficulty coping with the ups and down of everyday life.

As a result, teens might experience insomnia, or sleeplessness, constant stomachaches or headaches, or other health issues. Other problems can arise. Targets of bullying may drop out of school activities or sport teams. If young people feel unsafe, they could become afraid to

Teens who have a food allergy may become victims of bullying. Bullying is when someone or a group of people do or say hurtful things to gain power over another person.

go to school or perform poorly in their classes. Some people lose interest in friends and hobbies and have trouble making decisions and concentrating. Those who are depressed might abuse alcohol or other drugs or drive recklessly.

Teasing and bullying about a food allergy must be taken seriously. You can protect yourself, even in challenging situations. A good way to keep safe is to plan ahead so you will know what to do if you feel distressed or frightened. For instance, teens can ignore their teasers or explain how they feel and tell bullies to stop. If taunted with unsafe food in school, on school grounds, or during school-sponsored activities, young people can immediately leave the situation and get help. They can talk to a parent or another trusted relative or a school teacher, coach, nurse, or guidance

Dating often involves dining out. Teens who have a food allergy should be truthful with their date, rather than risk exposure to potential food allergens.

counselor. Many schools have antibullying programs that require school administrators to handle situations when bullying is reported.

Dating Fun

Dating can be fun and exciting! By going out in groups or with just one individual, teens get the chance to interact and feel comfortable with others. Meeting and spending time with a variety of people can help them learn the types of people they like and get along with best. It's also a time to practice communication and good decision-making skills.

However, dating can be stressful, particularly with the added concern of having a food allergy. To make socializing safer and more enjoyable, young people should talk openly about their food limitations with their date. Practicing what to say beforehand with a friend can help you feel more comfortable. It's best to give a brief explanation before getting together on the first date. You can describe what you can and cannot eat and which restaurants have safe options for you to choose.

Teens also need to tell their date that an allergic reaction can be severe, what symptoms to watch for, where their medications are, and what to do if a serious reaction happens. Most dates want to know the right steps to

SAFE SMOOCHING

When you do get ready to kiss, it's important that your date understands how serious your food allergy is and how to help keep you from having a reaction. If someone has recently eaten an allergen, like nuts, fish, or shellfish, kissing could cause a serious reaction. Even a quick peck on the cheek can result in a local reaction such as welts or hives, although it's highly unlikely to cause a severe response. Individuals who have eaten an allergy-causing food should brush their teeth, floss carefully, and wash their hands and face several hours before kissing. Both teens may want to follow the BRFW guidelines from Food Allergy Research & Education. BRFW stands for B—Brush Teeth, R—Rinse out the Mouth, F—Floss between Teeth, and W—Wait 4 Hours before Kissing. Or, preferably, your boyfriend or girlfriend will agree to avoid the food on days you will be together.

take if a problem arises. They will often ask questions, but may need some time to adjust to this aspect of your life. Someone who is willing to learn about your food allergy shows that he or she is worth getting to know better.

Young people may think that informing their date about a food allergy could ruin the chance of creating a romantic mood or enjoying the excitement of being together. But ending up in the emergency room is certainly no fun and not romantic for anyone. Staying safe by avoiding food allergens is a priority for everyone with a food allergy.

TEENS AND RISK

Teens and young adults with food allergies have the highest risk of fatal anaphylaxis compared to all other age groups. Many risk factors fuel this danger, including pressure from peers. Although peer pressure is normal, it's a powerful force that can push individuals toward making good or bad decisions. Most teens want to belong and be accepted by their friends. They do not want to be thought of as different from their peers because they fear ridicule or rejection.

As a result of wanting to fit in with friends, classmates, and other people, teens can behave recklessly and put themselves in risky situations. For example, they may eat unsafe food at school activities, parties, or other occasions to prevent feeling socially isolated or awkward. Sometimes young people purposely leave

Young people with a food allergy may feel calmer about a possible allergic reaction when their sports coach and team members understand what to do in case a problem occurs.

their autoinjectors or medical emergency identification at home so they dress and look like their peers. Students participating in sporting events want their teammates and competitors to view them as strong, capable, and invincible. To avoid looking weak, they may refuse to carry their medications on them during practice and games, and instead, stow the items in the gym locker room. Individuals may feel ashamed talking about their shellfish allergy with their date, for instance, and agree to eat at a seafood restaurant or fast-food place.

Sometimes young people turn to alcohol and other drugs as a way to cope with the added stress of managing a food allergy in their busy lives. However, using alcohol and drug lowers inhibitions and increases risk taking. As a result, teens could become careless about checking what they eat. Having any high-risk behaviors greatly increases the chance of consuming an unsafe food and causing an adverse reaction.

Taking responsibility for a food allergy involves learning how to cope with peer pressure. Being safe requires that young people make decisions that may be different from those of the group you are with or someone you want to impress. The more you practice developing good decision-making skills, the more likely you are to steer clear of problem foods and be prepared if emergencies do occur.

CHAPTER 8

BEING IN THE WORLD

Living with a food allergy is a significant concern every day. Eating at parties, in school or restaurants, or while traveling all need to be carefully planned beforehand. Teens living with food allergies quickly learn to be proactive with what they eat every day to stay safe, healthy, and happy.

CELEBRATE!

People enjoy coming together during holidays and at birthdays, graduations, and other parties. They usually celebrate with food, perhaps with special dishes, cake, ice cream, potlucks, or snacks like chips, salsa, trail mix, and candy. All the excitement can make it difficult to

Special events are often celebrated with delicious and fun foods. However, it's always wise to carry safe snacks in case none of the party food is acceptable.

be informed about ingredients at the festivities and may leave food-allergic teens wondering what to eat. By making some advance preparations, everyone can ensure their safety, which allows them to focus on having fun during social gatherings.

Before an event, young people can talk to the individual in charge by phone, by e-mail, or in person and explain their food allergy. Consider a short statement like, "I'm allergic to peanuts and tree nuts." It's OK to make several simple suggestions about safe foods for the party, such as fresh, seasonal fruit for snacks or dessert.

Other steps teens may take include shopping for or making allergy-free dishes or treats to bring to the occasion. Eating some allergy-friendly food beforehand or tucking safe snacks into a purse or bag can help them avoid tempting, but possibly harmful, food at a gathering. Before leaving the house, allergy sufferers should make sure to bring their medicines and wear their medical alert identification.

FRIENDLY RESTAURANTS

Eating at a restaurant can be challenging for teens with food allergies because they are always taking the risk of eating something they are allergic to. One way to handle these concerns is to learn about food ingredients and preparation. For example, some people with food allergies may need to avoid Asian, African, and Mexican dishes because they often include tree nuts, peanuts, fish, or shellfish.

A vast amount of information about food allergies, nutrition, and health is available in books, magazines, and newspapers, and on the Internet. However, some material is confusing or incorrect. When dealing with a food allergy, it's smart to find trustworthy sources and learn to judge the value of the advice before using it to make eating and lifestyle decisions. Identifying who runs a website is important. Web addresses that have the three-letter ending of .gov, .edu, or .org usually indicate credible sources. Quick, online assessments and counseling apps for smartphones, tablets, and other mobile devices can help teens keep track of their allergen triggers. Some apps include Allergen Free, Allergy & Gluten FreeScanner, AllergyEatsMobile, Food Allergy Detective, and My Food Facts.

FINDING RELIABLE INFORMATION ABOUT FOOD ALLERGIES

Before going out to eat, teens can locate a restaurant's website, find the menu, and look for several potential dishes. They might also call ahead or e-mail the restaurant's chef or manager, briefly explain their food allergy, and ask which menu items are safe. Even if the menu does not offer suitable dishes, individuals can ask whether a special meal can be prepared for them. Another option is to list dietary restrictions when making reservations.

At the restaurant, it's a good idea to speak with the wait staff or restaurant manager about your special food needs. You can present a chef card and ask that the chef review it. These cards list your allergy and explain that eating even a tiny bite of the food can make you very

sick. The Food Allergy Research & Education website offers a free chef card for anyone to complete online and then print. Many people laminate their cards to keep them protected from wear and tear, and make extra copies in case they forget their chef card at a restaurant.

Young people can question the restaurant staff about the ingredients in a dish or dessert and how the food is prepared before placing their order. For example, someone with peanut and tree nut allergies might ask, "Do these cookies contain peanuts, walnuts, almonds, or other nuts?" If the wait staff or chef does not know, it's best to choose another menu option. Keep in mind that plain, simple foods are usually allergen-free, such as baked regular or sweet potatoes, steamed vegetables, broiled chicken or meat, and fresh fruit. As a precaution, everyone can bring safe food to eat while they are at a restaurant with family or friends. Bringing your own food might feel uncomfortable at first, but it's a safe way to take care of yourself.

More and more restaurants are aware of food allergies and will accommodate people who have special needs. In addition, a growing number of fast-food chains provide allergy information on their websites, usually in a section labeled "Nutrition." Examples include Burger King, Culver's, Dairy Queen, Domino's Pizza, Kentucky Fried Chicken, McDonald's, Pizza Hut,

When eating out at a restaurant, don't hesitate to ask a busy host, hostess, or waitperson if certain foods are allergen-free.

Subway, Taco Bell, and Wendy's. Using smartphone apps such as AllergyEats, Allergy Free Restaurant Foods, and iCanEat Fast Food can also make eating out easier.

SAFE EATING AT SCHOOL

Most schools have a food allergy policy that specifies where a student's medications and emergency health care form are stored. Under the plan, teachers, nurses, cafeteria workers, coaches, and other school staff must be informed of the food allergy and what to do in an emergency. Many schools have allergy-free zones in their cafeterias where young people can safely eat with friends. The policy also covers sports, clubs, and other extracurricular activities.

On November 13, 2013, President Barack Obama signed the School Access to Emergency Epinephrine Act. This law gives students who have food allergies greater access to the drug by providing money to states that require their schools to provide epinephrine. Currently, only Maryland, Nebraska, Nevada, and Virginia mandate their schools to stock the medicine. State and local governments govern schools, not the federal government.

UP IN THE SKY

Many food-allergic people have flown around the United States and worldwide without a problem. You can, too, with some advance planning. To begin, it's essential to

Many people enjoy hiking, backpacking, and camping. If the group decides to have communal meals, everyone can plan an allergy-friendly menu in advance.

bring a carry-on kit that includes your antihistamines, autoinjectors, and food allergy emergency care plan. The Transportation Security Administration (TSA) requires that epinephrine remain in its original packaging with the printed label attached.

Savvy travelers also put their epinephrine prescription and a doctor's note that verifies their food allergy

It's not always easy to change what you like to eat, but by following an allergy-friendly diet, you will feel better and have more energy and enthusiasm to enjoy life.

in their kit. They should always keep any medications with them, not in an overhead bin. Everyone should wear his or her medical emergency identification and bring safe food to eat on the flight.

Before buying plane tickets, teens can read an airline's food allergy policy on its website. This information is located by typing "allergy" or "allergies" in the search box. Some airlines do not serve peanut snacks. Others offer pretzels, instead of peanut or nut snacks, upon advance request. People need to make arrangements for special meals on a flight beforehand. However, airlines cannot guarantee an allergen-free trip because passengers can eat any food they want on the plane.

LIVING TO THE FULLEST

Teens with a food allergy can do everything other teens do, except eat foods that trigger allergic reactions. Coping with a food allergy is a balancing act that affects every part of their daily life. They must avoid food allergens,

yet coexist with them at school, extracurricular activi-ties, and parties, or in other situations. Young people can take ownership of their food allergy by accepting responsibility for their condition. To stay safe, they must always be careful of what they eat. However, they can enjoy a wide variety of foods with family and friends.

Many people find that joining a support group is extremely helpful. Members share their experiences and knowledge and can gain useful advice and practical tips from other teens. It also helps to know you are not alone. To locate a food allergy support group, check with local health clinics, community centers, religious organizations, natural food stores, and print or online bulletin boards and newspapers. The Food Allergy Research & Education website offers local contact information for support groups across the country.

Coping confidently with food allergies and other challenges in one's life brings a sense of pride and self-assurance that can lead to success in many areas. It's essential to take care of your own well-being. This responsibility includes eating right and getting enough sleep. Regular exercise decreases stress, which boosts someone's mood and outlook on life. Do something you enjoy, such as jogging, hiking, swimming, skiing, or biking. Activities such as team sports or a brisk walk can help you feel good about yourself. People with food allergies can be as active as they want and live full and happy lives.

GLOSSARY

allergen A substance in the body that causes an allergic reaction.

allergist A doctor who specializes in diagnosing and treating people who are allergic to various things, including food.

allergy An overreaction of the immune system to a normally harmless substance, resulting in a rash, sneezing, coughing, breathing difficulties, or other symptoms.

anaphylaxis An extremely serious allergic reaction that affects the whole body and may cause breathing difficulties, fainting, or even death if not treated promptly.

antibody A protein (also called immunoglobulin) made by white blood cells in the body that fights against illness and infections.

antihistamine A drug used to block the effects of histamine, and, as a result, relieves allergy symptoms.

asthma A disease in which the air passages in the lungs become inflamed, making breathing difficult.

autoinjector A device with a needle used to put drugs into the body.

chronic Continuing for a long time or happening frequently.

cross-contamination When chemicals in one substance come into contact with another substance.

eczema A skin condition that causes redness, itching, and sometimes blistering.

epinephrine A medicine that helps to ease a severe allergic reaction.

food intolerance The inability to digest a particular food.

genetically modified organism (GMO) An organism in which the genetic code has been changed in laboratories.

genetics The study of how characteristics are passed on from parent to child.

hay fever An allergic reaction to pollen and dust, characterized by sneezing, a runny nose, and watery eyes.

histamine A chemical released by mast cells in the body that causes tissues to become swollen and inflamed.

hives Itchy, swollen bumps on the skin that are caused by an allergic reaction.

IgE antibody A chemical made in response to a first exposure to an allergen.

immune system The body's network of cells, tissues, and organs that work together as defense mechanisms against attack by foreign substances, such as bacteria and viruses.

mast cell A cell in the skin and the lining tissues, such as the breathing passages, that bind to IgE antibodies and release histamine during an allergic reaction.

pathogen A bacterium, virus, or other microorganism that can cause disease.

RAST test A blood test for specific kinds of IgE antibodies to show sensitivity to particular allergens.

respiratory system The lungs and airways that make breathing possible.

scratch test An allergy test in which a tiny amount of allergen is placed on a scratch to see if a skin reaction occurs.

sensitization The development of an allergy after exposure to an allergen.

vaccine A medicine given to protect someone from a specific disease.

white blood cell A blood cell that is an important part of the body's defense against harmful bacteria and viruses.

FOR MORE INFORMATION

Academy of Nutrition and Dietetics
120 South Riverside Plaza, Suite 2000
Chicago, IL 60606
Website: http://www.eatright.org

The Academy of Nutrition and Dietetics provides information on various aspects of food allergies.

Allergy/Asthma Information Association
21 Four Season Place, Suite 133
Toronto, ON M9B 6J8
Canada
(800) 611-7011
Website: http://www.aaia.ca

This association deals with all aspects of allergies, including food allergies, and provides resources for services and information.

AllergyKids Foundation
P.O. Box 3284
Boulder, CO 80307
Website: http://www.allergykids.com

The AllergyKids Foundation is a nonprofit organization that works to provide kids with safe affordable food free of additives often found in the food supply.

American Academy of Allergy, Asthma, and Immunology

555 East Wells Street, Suite 1100

Milwaukee, WI 53202-3823

(414) 272-6071

Website: http://www.aaaai.org

The AAAAI offers educational materials on food allergies, which are available by clicking the Patient Education link on the home page.

Anaphylaxis Canada

2005 Sheppard Avenue East, Suite 800

Toronto, ON M2J 5B4

Canada

(866) 785-5660

Website: http://www.anaphylaxis.ca

Anaphylaxis Canada offers practical strategies for living with anaphylaxis.

Asthma and Allergy Foundation of America

8201 Corporate Drive, Suite 1000

Landover, MD 20785

(800) 727-8462

Website: http://www.aafa.org

The Asthma and Allergy Foundation of America website provides food allergy information.

Food Allergy Research & Education

7925 Jones Branch Drive, Suite 1100

McLean, VA 22102

(800) 929-4040

Website: http://www.foodallergy.org

Food Allergy Research & Education works to keep people with food allergies safe and to find a cure for food allergies.

Food Allergy Research and Resource Program
143 Filley Hall
University of Nebraska-Lincoln
Lincoln, NE 68583-0955
(402) 472-7211
Website: http://farrp.unl.edu

This organization provides educational materials on food allergies, which are available by clicking the FARRP Resources link on the home page, and then clicking For Consumers.

Kids With Food Allergies (KFA)
5049 Swamp Rd, Suite 303
PO Box 554
Fountainville, PA 18923
Website: http://community.kidswithfoodallergies.org

Kids With Food allergies offers families and children useful food allergy information to help save lives and improve the quality of live for those who deal with allergies.

National Institute of Allergy and Infectious Diseases
5601 Fishers Lane, MSC 9806
Bethesda, MD 20892-9806
(800) 248-4107
Website: http://www.niaid.nih.gov

This agency conducts research to better understand, treat, and ultimately prevent allergic diseases.

U.S. Food and Drug Administration
10903 New Hampshire Avenue
Silver Spring, MD 20993
(888) 463-6332
Website: http://www.fda.gov
The Food and Drug Administration protects and promotes the public's health. Its website provides information on food allergies.

WEBSITES

Because of the changing nature of Internet links, Rosen Publishing has developed an online list of websites related to the subject of this book. This site is updated regularly. Please use this link to access the list:

http://www.rosenlinks.com/411/Food

Ballard, Carol. *Explaining Food Allergies*. Mankato, MN: Smart Apple Media, 2010.

Bellenor, Karen, ed. *Allergy Information for Teens* (Teen Health Series). Detroit, MI: Omnigraphics, 2013.

Bickerstaff, Linda. *Your Immune System: Protecting Yourself Against Infection and Illness* (Healthy Habits). New York, NY: Rosen Publishing, 2011.

Cain, Kenneth. *Nut Free? A Beginner's Guide to Living with Food Allergies*. Los Gatos, CA: Distressed Press, 2012.

Cooper, Alexandra DiRuscio. *So, What?!: A Teen's Guide to What Really Matters*. Seattle, WA: CreateSpace, 2011.

Esherick, Joan. *Managing Stress*. Broomall, PA: Mason Crest Publishers, 2013.

Food Allergies (Perspectives on Diseases and Disorders). Farmington Hills, MI: Greenhaven Press, 2013.

Ford, Jean. *Allergies & Asthma*. Broomall, PA: Mason Crest Publishers, 2013.

Francoeur, Laurel J. *Flying with Food Allergies: What You Need to Know*. Austin, TX: Greenlaurel Solutions, 2013.

Guillain, Charlotte. *Coping with Bullying*. Chicago, IL: Heinemann Library, 2011.

Gupta, Ruchi S. *The Food Allergy Experience: Black and White Edition*. Seattle, WA: CreateSpace, 2012.

Hand, Carol. *Living with Food Allergies*. Minneapolis, MN: Essential Library, 2012.

Hillstrom, Kevin. *Food Allergies*. Farmington Hills, MI: Lucent Books, 2012.

Kauke, Kristen W. *Growing Up Ben: Living a Full Life, With Food Allergies*. Seattle, WA: CreateSpace, 2013.

Koeller, Kim, Robert La France, and Alessio Fasano. *Let's Eat Out Around the World Gluten Free and Allergy Free*. New York, NY: Demos Health, 2014.

KIWI magazine. *Allergy-Friendly Food for Families: 120 Gluten-Free, Dairy-Free, Nut-Free, Egg-Free, and Soy-Free Recipes Everyone Will Enjoy*. Kansas City, MO: Andrews McMeel Publishing, 2012.

Peters, Rhonda. *So, What Can I Eat Now?!: Living Without Dairy, Soy, Eggs, and Wheat*. Lavenn, AZ: Rhonda's Cooking, 2010.

Rogers, Kara, ed. *The Digestive System* (The Human Body). New York, NY: Britannica Educational Publishing and Rosen Editorial Services, 2011.

Schwartz, Mireille. *The Family Food Allergy Book: A Life Plan You and Your Family Can Live With*. Columbus, OH: Basic Health Publications, 2013.

Skinner, Juniper. *Food Allergies and Me*. Seattle, WA: CreateSpace, 2010.

Snedden, Robert. *Understanding Food and Digestion* (Understanding the Human Body). New York, NY: Rosen Publishing, 2010.

Weissman, Susan. *Feeding Eden: The Trials and Triumphs of a Food Allergy Family*. New York, NY: Sterling, 2012.

Young, Michael C. *The Peanut Allergy Answer Book*. Minneapolis, MN: Fair Winds Press, 2013.

BIBLIOGRAPHY

Anca, Alexandra, and Gordon L. Sussman. *The Total Food Allergy Health and Diet Guide*. Toronto, Canada: Robert Rose, 2012.

Asthma and Allergy Foundation of America. "Facts and Statistics." Retrieved November 10, 2013 (http://www.aafa.org/display.cfm?id=9&sub=30).

Beaseley, Sandra. *Don't Kill the Birthday Girl: Tales from an Allergic Life*. New York, NY: Crown Publishers, 2011.

Bégin, Philippe. "Unproven and Non-Standardized Tests for Food Allergy." Food Allergy Research & Education. Retrieved November 18, 2013 (http://www.foodallergy.org/document.doc?id=238).

Duyff, Roberta Larson. *American Dietetic Association Complete Food Nutrition Guide*. Hoboken, NJ: John Wiley & Sons, 2012.

Food Allergy Research & Education. "About Food Allergies." Retrieved March 21, 2014 (http://www.foodallergy.org/allergens/other-allergens).

Food Allergy Research & Education. "Resources for Kids." Retrieved December 5, 2013 (http://www.foodallergy.org/resources/kids).

Food Allergy Research & Education. "School Access to Epinephrine." November 13, 2013. Retrieved January 3, 2014 (https://www.foodallergy.org/advocacy/school-access-to-epinephrine).

Gordon, Sherri Mabry. *Peanut Butter, Milk, and Other Deadly Threats: What You Should Know About Food Allergies*. Berkeley Heights, NJ: Enslow Publishers, 2006.

Hannaway, Paul J. *On the Nature of Food Allergy*. Marblehead, MA: Lighthouse Press, 2007.

Haupt, Angela. "How NFL Star Adrian Peterson Copes with Severe Food Allergies." *Daily News*, November 26, 2013. Retrieved December 10, 2013 (http://www.nydailynews.com/life-style/health/nfl -star-adrian-peterson-copes-severe-food-allergies -article-1.1529942).

Miller, Sloane. *Allergic Girl: Adventures in Living Well with Food Allergies*. Hoboken, NJ: John Wiley & Sons, 2011.

Oh, Chad K., and Carol Kennedy. *How to Live with a Nut Allergy*. New York, NY: McGraw-Hill, 2005.

Pawankar, Ruby, Giorgio Walter Canonica, Stephen T. Holgate, and Richard F. Lockey. "WAO White Book on Allergy 2011–2012: Executive Summary." World Allergy Organization. Retrieved November 10, 2013 (http://www.worldallergy.org/publications/ wao_white_book.pdf).

Rochman, Bonnie. "Bullying over Food Allergies." Time.com, December 25, 2012. Retrieved December 12, 2014 (http://healthland.time.com/2012/12/25/ bullying-over-food-allergies).

Sicherer, Scott H. *Food Allergies: A Complete Guide for Eating When Your Life Depends on It*. Baltimore, MD: John Hopkins University Press, 2013.

U.S. Centers for Disease Control and Prevention. "School Allergies." October 31, 2013. Retrieved November 10, 2013 (http://www.cdc.gov/healthyyouth/foodallergies).

U.S. Food and Drug Administration. "Food Allergen Labeling and Consumer Protection Act of 2004 Questions and Answers." July 18, 2006. Retrieved December 1, 2013 (http://www.fda.gov/food/guidanceregulation/guidancedocumentsregulatoryinformation/allergens/ucm106890.htm).

U.S. National Institute of Allergy and Infectious Diseases. "Guidelines for the Diagnosis and Management of Food Allergy in the United States: Summary for Patients, Families, and Caregivers." May 2011. Retrieved November 8, 2013 (http://www.niaid.nih.gov/topics/foodallergy/clinical/documents/faguidelinesexecsummary.pdf).

Wood, Robert A. *Food Allergies for Dummies.* Indianapolis, IN: Wiley Publishing, 2007.

World Health Organization. "20 Questions on Genetically Modified Foods." 2014. Retrieved November 23, 2013 (http://www.who.int/foodsafety/publications/biotech/20questions/en).

INDEX

A

additives, 22, 48, 69
Allergen Free, 87
allergens, 6, 10, 24, 58, 68
  and labeling foods, 31,
    68–70
  most common in food
    allergies, 6, 27–37, 69, 70
allergist, 33, 37, 46, 54, 56
  being diagnosed and tested
    by a, 7, 22–23, 38–45
  and emergency medical
    plan, 71, 91
  finding a knowledgeable, 46
  and medications, 50
  questions to ask a, 59
Allergy & Gluten
    FreeScanner, 87
AllergyEatsMobile, 87, 90
Allergy Free Restaurant
    Foods, 90
Allergy Journal, 45
American Academy of
    Allergy, Asthma, and
    Immunology (AAAAI),
    46, 71
American Board of Allergy
    and Immunology
    (ABAI), 46
American College of
    Allergy, Asthma, and

Immunology, 71
anaphylaxis, 16–17, 19, 32,
  33, 37, 41, 45, 81
  exercise-induced, 26
  handling, 50–54
antibodies, 10, 41, 42, 58
antihistamines, 50, 51–53,
  54, 56, 71, 91
applied kinesiology, 45, 47
apps, 45, 87, 90
asthma, 17, 50, 62
Asthma and Allergy
    Foundation of America,
    71
autoinjectors, 49, 51, 53,
  54–56, 71, 82, 91

B

Be a Pal program, 74
blood pressure, low, 4, 16
blood tests for allergies,
  40, 42
breathing, difficulty with, 4,
  50, 51, 53
BRFW guidelines, 80
bullying, 75–78

C

casein, 27, 29
celebrations, enjoying,
  84–86

About the Author

Judy Monroe Peterson has earned two master's degrees and is the author of numerous educational texts for young people, including books on the dangers of antidepressants, herbal drugs, steroids, nicotine, alcohol, and barbiturates. She is a former health care, technical, and academic librarian and college faculty member; a biologist and research scientist; and curriculum editor with more than thirty years of experience. Currently, she is a writer and editor of K–12 and post-high school curriculum materials on a wide variety of subjects, including health, nutrition, biology, life science, and the environment.

Photo Credits

Cover, p. 1 Alliance/iStock/Thinkstock; pp. 4–5 photka/Shutterstock.com; pp. 8–9 Igor Mojzes/iStock/Thinkstock; pp. 12–13 andreasnikolas/Shutterstock.com; p. 15 Dr. P. Marazzi/Science Source; pp. 20–21 JGI/Jamie Grill/Blend Images/Getty Images; p. 23 Tom Myers/Science Source; pp. 24–25 gourmetphotography/Shutterstock.com; pp. 28–29 smereka/Shutterstock.com; p. 30 Olinchuk/Shutterstock.com; p. 34 Marie C Fields/Shutterstock.com; p. 36 Tom Dahlin/Getty Images; p. 39 Camille Tokerud/Iconica/Getty Images; pp. 40–41 Southern Illinois University/Photo Researchers/Getty Images; p. 43 Daniel Grill/Getty Images; p. 52 mario loiselle/E+/Getty Images; pp. 54–55 Andy Ryan/Taxi/Getty Images; p. 57 Ian Boddy/Science Source; pp. 60–61 Monkey Business Images/Shutterstock.com; pp. 62–63 Blend Images/Moxie Productions/Vetta/Getty Images; pp. 66–67 Fuse/Getty Images; p. 69 Peter Dazeley/Photographer's Choice/Getty Images; pp. 72–73 Eric Raptosh Photography/Blend Images/Getty Images; pp. 76–77 Christopher Futcher/E+/Getty Images; pp. 78–79 John Giustina/The Image Bank/Getty Images; p. 82 Rana Faure/Photodisc/Getty Images; pp. 84–85 Klaus Vedfelt/Taxi/Getty Images; p. 88 Comstock/Stockbyte/Thinkstock; p. 91 Ascent Xmedia/The Image Bank/Getty Images; pp. 92–93 Marc Romanelli/Blend Images/Getty Images.

Designer: Les Kanturek; Editor: Heather Moore Niver; Photo Researcher: Karen Huang